RUN FOR THE SHADOWS

Sridala Swami is a poet, essayist and photographer. Her first collection of poems, *A Reluctant Survivor* (2007), was shortlisted for the Shakti Bhatt First Book Award in 2008. It was followed by *Escape Artist* (2014), which was shortlisted for the inaugural Khushwant Singh Poetry Prize. Her work has featured in *The Bloodaxe Book of Contemporary Indian Poets* (2008).

Sridala was the 2011 Charles Wallace writer-in-residence at the University of Stirling, Scotland, and was a Fellow of the International Writing Program at the University of Iowa, 2013. In 2020 she was on the jury of the Montreal International Poetry Prize.

She has also written four books for children. Some of these books have been translated into many languages, including Polish, French and Korean.

RUN FOR THE SHADOWS

SRIDALA SWAMI

cntxt

First published by Context, an imprint of Westland Publications Private Limited, in 2021

Published by Context, an imprint of Westland Books, a division of Nasadiya Technologies Private Limited, in 2022

No. 269/2B, First Floor, 'Irai Arul', Vimalraj Street, Nethaji Nagar, Allappakkam Main Road, Maduravoyal, Chennai 600095

Westland, the Westland logo, Context and the Context logo are the trademarks of Nasadiya Technologies Private Limited, or its affiliates.

ISBN: 9789395073387

10 9 8 7 6 5 4 3 2 1

Typeset in ArnhemFine Regular by SÜRYA, New Delhi

Printed at Manipal Technologies Limited, Manipal

for

Jayanta Mahapatra & Keki N. Daruwalla

and for

Kasturi & Swayambhu

To live past the end of your myth is a perilous thing.

– Anne Carson

CONTENTS

RUN FOR THE SHADOWS

DEAR STRANGER DECIPHERING THIS ANCIENT SCRIPT

Dear stranger, dear sentient being from a future so far I cannot imagine anything about it:

not the shape of poems
not the way you will handle the corners
of pages
not the science you will use to decipher
this ancient script in which I write but which to me is given and taken for granted,

Dear stranger who makes my work timeless and immortal, for whose eyes only
I seal this message in the bottle of centuries,

Dear salvager, dear rescue artist, dear hauntologist:

What have you done?

I wrote to escape attention. There was a brief sentence I had to serve before remembrance could be not about what has been. I wanted to fall like dust and be renewed in leaves.

How much have you forgotten?

I would like these words to be like a child's first drawings. If you must, keep them as you would a stone you picked to remember a place you visited.

Dear stranger, I say these things because I know they will mean nothing to you.

BLESSING

– for Swayambhu

The year we became still and hid
in plain sight like river stones
ground grey
hoping nothing would touch us
good or evil
dreams walked hand in hand
with nightmares

and even you, who arrowed your way
back into this nest
must have dreamt of flight
since it also is an unsettling

We hunkered down
like roots in winter
we gathered together
like distressed trees
signalling for help   we gave succour
to each other from the unseen places.

There will be a later.

There will be a later that holds hope
the way the screeching kite
        is held aloft by all of the air.

When the time comes
even fledglings move from
        effort into lightness

And you, for whom
I still dream of flight
when the time comes
        though you are now tightly held

when the time comes
        may you be slowly released

when the time comes
        may you rise into hope

when the time comes
        may you find the world
        in that vast kindness.

DREAM: MIDNIGHT

He is twelve
and is to be executed by drowning.
He escapes.
Now he is sitting in front of me as if he has just come
out of a shower
but he is shivering.
I have no time to hold him
or release the grief that held me.
I must hide him
from the full house that is
half-emptied of what it holds.
A cardboard wall, hardly enough.
It must suffice. For now.
The people know he is here
but they greet him as if he had never left
and never needed to.
I still do not know what he did.
Like every mother I say, 'My son is innocent.'

How did they plan his execution?
Is it all make-believe?
Were they pirates? Did they make him walk
the plank? Did he walk off the edge
like a fool
with his head in the clouds?
I can believe this last
But I cannot believe in execution by drowning.
It is not civilised.
It is not how we live
where we live.
There weren't men lined up, rifles pointed
at the boy who came up for air
and reached right for the clouds.

He flew. This is what occurs to me.
I still dream of flight
as if the bowl of heaven is an illusion
just because I can see right through it.
I gave him wings but he used them to come home.
Twelve is too young to be thinking of nests,
too old for a son and his mother.

He cannot be drowned
though he can no longer fly.
But he can dream of flight
and perhaps that was enough
to bring him out of the water
as if it was an inverted bowl
without substance.

IDLE BLISS

after Auden

I am transcribing the sunshine.
The river flows backwards and the sky
borrows the light from it.

I fall upwards, a returning spacewalker
in free fall.
There is no land.

This is idle bliss: to plunge
and never land, to jump
and meet only cloudy ocean.

To forget the moment before
                lose the effort
            and become cloud

carrying its own sun within
lit, idle, eliding effort for fun.

ROMANCE, WITH CARNATIC VOCAL

Kanna, these gestures the rain makes
it makes for you
first as violin then as kanjira.
It was meant to be —
intensely —
        (but the rain forgets it falls
         as lightning does)

it was meant to be – not like rainbows
that never knew
they were on view
or they might have dressed
for the occasion

– romantic   like the kurinji
which comes rarely, comes suddenly
and brings no edges when it does
and instigates nothing in its name.

Kanna —
what will the girl sing
who sings to her friend about him
as she waits

for when he walks down the street
and the streetlights
drop their orange flowers at his feet

flowers she will later pick and thread
into unfading, solar-powered garlands
of kanakambaram?

Will she sing in five notes
tremolos and gamakas
falling jaltarangily?

Will her love be needles
Kanna,
because you didn't come
when you said you would
(because you forget
like the lightning)?

Or will her voice be
like dancing
sweet clap of arched feet
on smooth grey concrete
the smell of armpits and necks
and smudge-streaked foreheads?

Kanna, these gestures
are theories.
When you meet
forget rain
forget streets, feet, flowers.

Listen: there's a tillana playing
that you already know.
Keep time
the way she keeps it
until you return.

FORENSIC FLOWERS

In the neologisms of the future

we will need words for fossils formed
    from compressed glass
and plastic on the beach
        phrases for landfills of digital waste.

We will make dolorous words for mercury
    metamorphosed from bulbs
into glittering flowers
        fallen to dust.

There will be names – grand ones –
    for the shapes
embedded within the bellies of whales
        pregnant with dreck and scrap.

We'll trip over the petroglyphs that remain
    after the things that took flight
left only shadows behind
        burned into the ground's memory.

There will be planet-sized museums
and dictionaries enough, work enough
for a world turned over
            to patient excavation.

We can be bards, midwives, lexicographers.
            We can be gods intoxicated
by the ravaged sobriety
      of new forms
            birthed into being.

[THIS THING CALLED PEACE]

I read about war to avoid this thing
called peace hovering uneasily over our days.

The planes prowl the dark skies seeking
places people can't find on a map.

Afterwards, the story-telling:
it's simple, it's complicated.

As the day moves from longitude to longitude
the world moves from peace to peace

following the drums
of war or justice, it's hard to tell which.

CONQUEST OF PARADISE

After all, the apples continued to grow upon the trees
as they did after every conquest.

They ripened in the autumn sun dreaming
their own idylls.

It's a kind of paradise to go on as before
though the presiding gods come and go —

to live as if the midnight knocks were a worm growing
inside a fruit gone bad right from its tender time

as if stones weighed on the scales against bullets
were the same as objects bouncing off bodies

instead of invading them and then, once there, scattering
like untimely hail upon a harvest

pocking the skin and keeping the more severe damage
hidden inside.

The land but not the people: this ever inventive path
to suffering.

A land without the people might be either the orchard without
the gun leaning against the wall

or a child turning the barbed-wire corner of some nightmare
and never returning;

which people, whose absence will let these rivers
these mountains

this very air, crisp as some rich country's autumn
return to its reverie

of harvest and plenty, of enough and more, of a varied richness
from which no dreamer would want to wake?

The stone or the bullet to chase away
this kind of person or that?

The two things are not equal and never have been:
but conquerors have always known this

though sometimes they also know to hide this knowledge
like a secret worm

at the heart of the apple they permit to grow upon the trees
from which *these* people

the conquered, continue to pluck and keep a few,
keep the enchantment alive.

RITUALS OF DEPARTURE

'The first desire will accompany you to the last breath.'

– Etel Adnan

For years I thought of nothing but my father's death and the manner of its arrival: the prognosis so sudden and dramatic, the lingering decade when we treated the disease like an honoured guest that we wouldn't allow to leave, coddling it, and later accompanying it as it made to depart, dreading the lives that would be uprooted by the force of its final departure, as it was said the trees uprooted themselves to follow Hanuman as he took off for Lanka, not wanting to be parted from him but falling back to earth after all, as they must, and having to live with the consequences of the violence, and its aftermath.

We were ravaged but we recovered. Years later, when my own body began to alert me to its impermanence, I ignored it. Other people needed my attention more and I gave it. My body, insistent, showed me where it would give. Was I surprised that in this matter it followed my father? The path was already familiar. Death would come but could it not be invited in, the customs and forms of its welcome already in place and no surprises along the way? It may not have been what I had desired but in this particular avatar it was a companion I was familiar with. I could be a courteous host to this old guest leave when it does, quietly and in silence, just as my father did.

MY MOUTH IS BORED

Every fried, spiced morsel settles upon my liver, dissolves into globules of fat
and coats this large organ with dots of yellow.

Is it grey on the inside like the ultrasound tells me it is? Livid? What colour is calm?
What do organs look like when medical eyes are not upon them?

I remember the quarterly endoscope that my father swallowed, its merciless path down
past the bumps in the oesophagus where food lay like plaque.

Not everything that enters the body leaves it; some things remain untransmuted
unsightly when discovered. The inside is not designed to be seen.

Every night, like my father who tucked a handful of peanuts in his dhoti before settling
in front of the tv, I raid the kitchen a couple of hours after dinner.

I'm not hungry; it's my mouth that's bored. It craves not food but sensation.
It wants to water like I want to cry
but it's easier to make the one thing happen than the other.

If I take time over this snack maybe it will go through my liver
instead of making a permanent home upon it.
To be safe, I do a few quick leg raises then sit in vajrasana.

When the endoscopy was over my father and I used to order food
in the hospital canteen: pongal dripping with ghee. Upma. Soft food, not too spicy
the peppers and green chillies picked out and left to the side.

My indiscriminate mouth can water even at the most painful memories
if there are spices involved.
Sometimes my eyes join in.
The late-night snack makes this plausible.

DIVINATION

Two days into life's last quarter, I look back at yesterday as if it was long ago.
In the scheme of things, the time I had and the time left to me
yesterday might as well have been a long time ago
and with the perfection of hindsight I can see that it began badly.

The signs were there: the overheating body, the fingers like little balloons
or empty surgical gloves unanimated by flesh and mind. I am saying
the accident may have been inevitable. Another sign:
the sense of anticipation of plans made – looking ahead with pleasure.

This is how the unexpected and the unwelcome make a home somewhere
at the back of the rib cage, unreachable yet ever-present, unpleasant.
This is me making a soft house for dread around my waist.
I carry my future within my body, as I always have, but more consciously now.

Other people's broken bones and lives changed in an instant, a shock
to my system. This is selfishness at work, looking for lessons in misfortunes —
anyone's will do so long as I am involved even slightly. It could have been me.
I don't want it to be me, or my loved ones, not ever. I want all the luck

and I want it to never run out and I want it to bless everyone I point it at
like a holy censer, an ever-replenished balm, a fountain of all that could
go wrong but didn't
        and I still don't know how it will end but I want it to be sudden and final.

SWALLOWING SILK

That fan again, dangerous and low
your voice beating the air
shaking the dust down upon us
these cane-backed chairs and art deco tiles.

The tea is orange, skinned over.
I coat my tongue with a thick silence
watch the world go by
out the two exits here.

You talk while I put on my listening face
the one I perfected in the first row
of every classroom I've ever been in.
A notebook would make me look even more attentive.

There's a glass of water on the table.
The forensic light shows up
fingerprints. I run a finger down the side
erasing another person as I go.

Outside, cycles and scooters
tilt into each other
as if nothing more important
will ever happen to them again.

You wind down.
The fan beats in the silence.
I sip water from the glass.
It tastes of camphor.

I am swallowing silk
and the distance we unfurled today
I fold it all away
and put it in fragrant storage.

LIKE LIGHT

The magic of air and light water and soil
things that permeate and things that refract
and the person who lets everything through
whole and unaltered who shifts the landscape
by being in it

It streams before and after and the person
like a loom that weaves nothing holds briefly
all things as they pass   leaves no impress
unless as a memory that because unseen
is a kind of magic

A still stone moves as fast as a wind
when it is unfixed in a consciousness
that lets everything through like light

What remains
An electric relay racing
out of one form into another growing
changing falling the rot and the revival
the sheer the energetic the incremental
teeming through emptiness.

SMOKE, FIRE

I.

A thought:
always the daisy
never the chain.

*

A string of them —
        pearls beyond price.

*

Shorter than believed
        the dimension of the present
thought.

*

A word thought
vs
A sentence thought.

*

Who would have thought
   And yet —
who would have thought?

*

So much blood
   in a thought
   in a word.

What was I thinking?

II.

What was I thinking?

I was thinking how hard it is to hold on to the world
just through thinking about it. I was thinking
in whole sentences but the words stopped cooperating.

Before I knew it, the world fell apart.
It took a few months.

How many thoughts in a month?
What is the distance between thoughts
And is it to be measured in time or space?

I don't know how to hold on
to what I know or seek what I don't.

ARRIVAL

A young man in a cold building is filled with silence.
The opening salvo a bird invisible, a small movement
in the grass. *Alone* on a human scale, *solo* on a class scale.
Someone gives him a breakfast made of old things.
The air is cold but not stale. He is the freshening. It comes alive.
The steps sing upwards. What it is to have all this, all this
all for oneself, the secret everyday desire for everything, exclusively.
The young man fills the silence with heat expanding.
For a whole day and a whole night he is *seule*
except for the voices at the other end, except for the life
of the night, except for the silent creatures in the corners
and cracks of all the rooms he cannot occupy by himself.
This particular moment. This before.
A young man revels in it, breathes it in for all it's worth —
one brief moment, a deep drawn breath
until he arrives, finally, at sleep, warm in his solitude, the night
left out in the cold with all those whose arrival is yet
to take particular form: this conveyance, that storied journey
the other companion who could not make it in time.

ALL THAT IS SOLID

Deep under the ground where dead things are kept
but not preserved   he goes to retrieve that which has kept
on decaying   believing what is under the earth is kept
pristine   a place of storage merely even preservation   a crypt

that honours memory while he descending is alive to secure
reassurance: that things stay the same in the cold and dark   secure
from the depredations of time so that even he – as he is – insecure
bag of flesh   animated corpse in the half light – the word *sarco*

phagus intrudes upon the matter that composes his thinking mind —
how can an object meant to preserve the physical body even though the mind
has fled   be called *flesh-eating*? – so that even he *claustrophobic* would not mind
being interred when his time comes —
                his tangled thoughts turn   he turns lightwards – breathturned –

to all that is solid and in the air and warm buoyant alive
(keeps for another time the thought of the things that live
burrowing) all that hurts and ages quickens and enlivens
he   keeper of the dead   returns above   a haunting of lyric.

SPIRIT ANIMAL

– for Amma

You recognise that moment when one part of you ribbons out
to reside in the animal that came seeking something that you
were willing to give.

You gave more and you've never been sure
if that also was sought and you just didn't know at the time —
but the giving has made you young and the creature strong.

She sits curled on the wall or the sill, belly full
an assumed dignity that comes more easily with practice.
She is goddess, she is Bastet – and sometimes she remembers it.

She was the runt of the litter but she was intrepid. And so
she was named. Needed help but accepted it
as nothing more than her due.

You watch and maybe you learn: how to accept without
undue gratitude; how to be fearless or at least how to fake it;
and how to fold antic youth within the stature of your age.

She teaches you detachment, a still and watchful patience,
endless grace. But there's always something left to learn: how to
sharpen your claws, land on your feet and find new lives to live.

BARTHES TELLS THE STORY WRONG

If you want definitions, here is one: a lover is one who waits.

The next part, the part where definitions are unwoven and the threads laid bare, can be left to Barthes, Roland, who said everything about it that needs to be said. And for what cannot be (and there are still some of those things) there are films, which – no matter what the structuralists say – are not to be *read*.

BARTHES

There was a girl who sat every evening at a particular table, hoping it was close enough to where the boys sat to make it appear a natural veering off when (if) he came to sit at it, opposite her; but not close enough to make her seem desperate.

Not always was her waiting played out as gestures of solitude. Other people gave her company. There was nothing in her face that could be read as signs of biding. This did not mean that she knew her time was up. This did not mean that she ceased to wonder and hope and despair and curse.

This is where Barthes got the story of the mandarin wrong, the one who pined for the courtesan who had said that after the 100th night of waiting, she would be his. What Barthes did was to report the mandarin's departure on the penultimate night. He didn't say how, on the night the mandarin left, the courtesan had made up her mind to tell him he'd waited enough, he could come in and

instead

she waited.

RB: 'Waiting', *A Lover's Discourse*

THE REFRACTIVE INDICES OF WORDS

The road between clarity
and obscurity
is paved with
the refractive indices of words.

My crystal your mud.
My harvest your husk.
My papier your mâché.

Not erasure but bending.
The thought like

lighght

approaching at speed
until
the brakes are applied.

DREAM: DAWN

In the kind of dream that comes with sleep rather than the kind one keeps
as a buttress against the future I buy back two of my own dresses from
a street-side shop where the clothes are hung against blue plastic as advertisement
and ware. I lost these clothes along with much else when that relationship ended.
You could even call it a nightmare and you would be right because the paths
to the shops are twisted and there are men whose intentions must be suspect
even in dreams because that is how deep warning bells sound even in the silence
of sleep. Things reach for me. They could be hands or voices but they have
the same weight.

I buy my own dresses back without telling the man they were always mine
and I wrap them around my hands. I build myself back. Another man offers
to show me the way out of the maze and though I know, somewhere outside
the dream-state, that I should pick a side and follow it to the end whether deeper
inside or out beyond this decrepitude held under the crown of an ancient banyan,
this knowledge is beyond me in the dream and besides there's a smell of khaki
about this man playing guide and I can't remember if I am to trust it or not.
My instinct says not.

At last there's a woman but she ignores me because she's on the phone and – this
is an old dream, by which I mean the objects and practices in it
are from decades ago – the phone is in an STD booth. The display is red
and changing fast, beyond what my own meagre purse contains and I feel anxious
for her, for myself. There's not enough time. There are so many incomplete tasks
I fear the dream will not allow me to complete: my scattered life
the way out of here and all the absences I haven't begun to account for.

THE MUSE GRIEF

Do you hate more the way you used your grief
to feed your muse and fuel your art
or do you hate the thing itself
without which there might have been
more ebb than flow in the clear waters
of your inspiration?

The triggers are everywhere and you remove
all the content warnings that might help you
steer clear of the stabs that are sure to wound
and keep the wound bleeding clear and clean
and the tide of the art flowing.

Luckily for you that state of forgetting the self
that the world calls happiness is in short supply
and the neurotically diverse ways of imagining
the end of things spring from the most unlikely
sources: song lyrics, the unsynchronised rise
and fall of garden life and – really, how hard
people try to keep going

and you just have to breathe it all in
feel it fill you and call it inspiration
that elusive thing you want to hold on to
beyond the last breath, beyond the body's
capacity to keep air captured as if it were
a bird or a hamster in a cage
pouring its panic and grief endlessly
in circles always and forever.

DIALOGUE

What lasts?

What speaks?

Tongues fail
Paper burns.
Even stone is beaten into silence by the elements.
Words themselves are inconstant.

Therefore, what lasts?

The language of stone. The language of blood and bone.
Inside, everyone is bilingual.

What remains?

Entrails. Read them. Read faces in repose, birds in flight, the
ache in bones, the circles in trees, smoke signals that
factories send out. Read the foam and the echo.

Everything must be constantly watched
lest a few hours change the world beyond all recognition.

It is not that I want you to hope...

It comes anyway, an uninvited guest.
I ask for love and I am sent hope.

Hope never speaks. Love is voluble, even prolix.
Not half the things we hear need ever have been spoken.

What speaks?

Reproductions.

Reproductions ... speak.

The original is always a question. Reproductions are replies.

So language is a souvenir we take away to remind us of the thought?

The night unmakes me. I am a reproduction of who I was yesterday.
Same but different.

The self is discontinuous. Or it can be discontinued.

Untied.

Unbundled.

Scattered.

Pirated Pirated
torrented torrented
distributed distributed
'*to live past the* end of your myth.'

VERTICAL SMILE

I'm smiling at you a vertical smile
dark like nothing you've ever seen
Smile back please Sing into my mouth
Draw out my breath as you would a ribbon
sliding it between your fingers Tie me
to you tie you to me Now breathe

Stay this way Hold this smile between
your lips until it is no longer a gesture but
a memory lodged in muscle & blood re-
call in later years these hours when
more than blood called when what gave
answer was something we could not name

Then forget all this because this is a
vertiginous fall Step back from the brink

now

MELODRAMA

Sometimes you just need a couple of quickly sketched-in scenes
for after, during which the reader can recover her composure;
a little time after the bodies have been cleared, the wounds cleaned
and dressed, the lovers left to sleep it off, when you can let words
wash over you, a little extra cleansing, a little no-time, a little
mint to let the palate recover. Because at the height of all the drama
you felt the tightness in the belly, the urge to let the tears flow,
you needed the catharsis of all these people being cruel to each other
using their words to wound and they did, they wounded you
and you welcomed it. It was a job neatly done but after all
the recovery room is also real and someone must occupy it and all
the dramatis personae have their own places and you must have yours.
Therefore that extra time, that spacious room of nothing much:
maybe a little light conversation, someone clearing a closet
or tending to a garden or sitting in a train watching the fields go by
counting animals, collecting odd signs, thinking, smiling a little
at nothing in particular. Listen for that long breath slightly shuddering:
the sound of satisfaction, that moment when nothing more
is needed to fill the immediate future because the story is still present
and it is enough.

IF THE SEA

with a first line from Carl Phillips' 'Cortege'

If the sea could dream, and if the sea
dreamt rain in reverse it would rise
in lines vertical dashes
erasing the air as it went.

If the salt in the sea could dream
it would dream of blood
vessels slowing current
damaged heart of the warming ocean.

If, when the waves dream
they are the thoughts of the drowning,
they stun themselves into clarity
and become sea glass.

If the creatures of the sea dreamt
of containment and spilling
of conquest over land and sky
what would they plant and how would it grow?

If the sea could dream
of hiding and scintillation
it would put down roots into the sacred floor
anchored until awake.

ANNOTATIONS

Between the incantations of flowers
Zinnia, wisteria, begonia, balsam
        Tecoma, tabebuia, bauhinia, saptaparni
between beds of future *eggplants*
and in the spaces between the *jerul*'s leaves
that live simultaneously in two seasons

in these spaces I plant the names
myrtle cedar willow sycamore
these stones carry their distant perfume
fig and *citron*, *walnut* and *birch*
I place them like footnotes and citations
on the margins of this garden

feed it the mulch of nomenclature
aspidistra saxifrage kurinji
        samphire rockweed sea grass
a whiff of salt and snapping air
trapped and transported in these shells

placed along the river stones bordering
cuphea, vadamalli, duranta, geranium
kanakambaram skies fallen
among the absent *peony* and the
gentian the *edelweiss* and the *takhellei*

blatant invitations to
the hiveminders and the dreamers
who can imagine the whole
know how to graft what is not there
into what is with the barest extracts.

THE TENDERNESS OF BEING TWO

after Sartre's letter to Beauvoir

To know that
though far away
you are the reason I spin
in this direction
like this.

I am
aloneless
unstrung song
serial
like notes
not notation

never on the same page
but bookending silence
sometimes so small
we touch across
that time.

RELAXATION TIME

Give a number a name and mountains will flow.
Nothing is solid, least of all water. It is all states
all boundaries. Before god
before the sunne, the air, warmth, before
splendour. It is slow, slower than life,
without season or strife, it takes all things as it goes.

There are no auguries in rivers when all things
are river. All things the sea. The sea is homeless.
The mountains have melted. All names
are taken and then taken away, drowned.
Give the drowning a number. Still it will
be the only thing called home.

SLOW, RIVER

River —
step away from the shore.
Your end
is around the next bend.

Skirt around
your island daughters —
they are blood
you are water.

Time moves
like you.
Slow down.
Make it pass.

Run slow, river
retreat underground
hide in plain sight

in the sky among the stars
a stream in an ocean.
An empty bed in which to die of thirst.

SCENE

A forest is in thought.
Branches are unresolved.
Birds are leaves in motion.

Inattention, careful, and then —

A forest is a stereogram.
Birds in dolby surround.
Movement, like the sky, invisible.

In repetition there is no pattern —

A forest is clarity.
Without the attention.
Birds, branches, sky, intent.

IF WINTER COMES

Can we have winter now?
Can we have the impossible cold
that freezes hell over —
the kind of threat of *never*
that is bound to be so meaningless
it practically means
not until next month at least.

If winter were to come next month
I would make the kind of promises
that are easy to keep.
I would promise food for frost
because the earth is saturated
and it would cost me nothing
to let the cold take hold.

When winter arrives like a big cat
stalking prey, disguising its darkness
amidst the gold of the still bright sun
I will surround myself with the warmth
of the oven and the fire, not as talisman
but as bait – to give it something
it wants to devour.

Give us a winter long in the tooth
but determined to stay. Though
the cubs and lambs may frolic together
in the spring may that regeneration
be far in the future, stopped in its tracks
by the slow dreaming of ice, frost and snow
a time so interminable it seems permanent.

DREAM: NOON

How seamlessly the dream moved
from what it was
to what I wanted it to be

and how very much the same
they were in
their elusiveness:

the waking mind
as slippery
as the sleeping one

each taking
the same route
to a different destination.

CINEMA PATHÉ

One night we walked back from our weekly screenings   it was cold and I had a shawl   a moon as big as a cliché dangled over the bare treetops   our reluctance to part   watching for the approach of teachers hiding behind their flashlights   we were innocent

beware! beware!

My shirt was ripped down the side though you didn't know it and you would never find out   the film may not have been lousy but I left   my open shirt   and a few minutes later

you followed me out and past the lab and the sundial to the benches by the basketball court

yardarms are for hanging

there were leaves   the rubble they turned into   constant and inflammable

(the story goes that truck drivers carrying fuel drove recklessly because they thought the word *inflammable* meant *that which was incapable of catching fire*)

Truly unruly rural unreal

no smoke, no fire, no rumours, no retreat, no surrender, no morning after the night before

I told you: we were innocent.

[This is where the titles roll.]

MONTAGE ON LOVE

*

When he leaves, she is condensed by shock until, like a seed, she becomes the original of herself.

*

For her it was hard to be in love again. It put her under serious pleasure.

*

He was irresistible as only the very young of any species are programmed to be. He played enthusiasm like an extreme sport.

*

No, he did not play. He imagined. The two things are different only because of outcomes.

*

Somewhere outside this paradise (which is, after all, nothing but an enclosed garden) are places where outcomes are not surrounded by walls. She wonders what to call the things that are placed in paradise.

*

She considers inoculating herself against future shock by administering small, daily doses of loss. Against her better judgement, she finds she has become a hoarder.

*

He also was a hoarder but a stealthier one. What he hoarded and where he stored it are enduring secrets.

*

It was always difficult to say *they*. It is a word that did not come easily to either of their tongues.

*

But that is not why she left. [Why he left.] That was an act of superb, of beautiful disentanglement.

*

She condenses. He deliquesces. Incoherence and silence are not the same thing. Hoarding and holding are not the same thing.

SATORI

How much the future is like a helmet
when it smashes into me.
I have turned a corner and my body
is soft.

Round and routed —
                I am unprepared
a candle just blown out.

As fire fixes clay
age has fixed me
and it's fixed me good.

PERIMENOPAUSAL

After the migraine after the assault
of smells
    burning leaves
    pillow covers
    food
    metals
after the sickness on the tongue and the body's slow dilation

the uterus gives a tug
    as upon a tampon cord

and —

O wouldn't it be wonderful
if a single tug birthed
    this egg
whole and small and perfect as a bud

  blood in zero gravity

a last delicate offering

to the crone waiting
to come
into her own.

AGAINST THE GRAIN

Sleep comes like a blunt instrument
in the days before.
Rothko behind afternoon eyes.
Colours pulse.
The agitated horizontal.

Parallaxed, a third kind of eye.
It turns inward.
Words run, chased by
a pill wielding sleep.
Struck
        I vibrate
horizontal and unquiet.

HYPOTHETICAL

The stinging lip
The ringing ear
The toppled light

This is not hypothetical.

If you could kill with your bare hands,
you said   *bare hands*
the one you love
and the world became a better place —

this is hypothetical.
A better world in words only.

If you acted if you did not act
If you rose if you drowned
If you stayed or left
If you were staid or deft
If you sliced time too thin for pain
If you provided a line and turned it into a rope
If you allowed yourself to hope
If you spidered into a corner

If you drew and quartered
If you cornered truth and flayed it alive
If you were surrounded by light
If your blind spot shone like a torch in the dark
If you loved with your bare hands
If you stung with your lips
If you toppled the light with your blind spot
If you drowned with your wings
                                        If you stopped
If you walked away.

All your life, hypothetical.

'DANCING IS A HEADLESS THING'

All summer I watch him dance, this liquid child.

It is a season of urgent distraction, urgent attention.
There is so much too much and none of it is happening
to me   and I am glad and guilty in equal measure.

All spring I watched him speak only with his eyes.

Elsewhere there was wailing unceasing
and the least we could do – the very least – was to listen, keep watch.
The numbers grew then thinned then clustered into dangerous spaces.

When the rains came, the statues fell.

I understand dance differently now:
the unselfing of it, the mind detached, the memory
lingering only in muscle and movement.

It is winter when he learns detachment.

So many ways to be headless:
they danced a gathering
they called for the guillotines
there were no leaders
they became water
they were held and held
there were no dancers left.

HUNGER STONES

– Wenn du mich siehst, dann weine

The stones appeared after all but they were not under the ground
or revealed gradually in a slowly creeping disaster no one noticed
until it was upon them.

Suddenly they were there.
They dragged at the feet of children
crying to be picked up because they'd walked too long
on too little.
Men and women, young and old, carried stones
for rations as they walked back to a place
they called home.

When the stones appeared the people were cleaved.
It was the hunger. It was vast,
vast as the stores of grain hoarded
against just such a day,
a day people long ago prepared for
but now that day had arrived
the hoard had turned to rot.

The stones appear
when the living can no longer imagine
even the present.

When you see them, then weep.

MEDITATION

Sitting in my cone of silence
watching hope work its way
through and past me
like fear in that litany.

In high summer
I tend the garden early
news of water flies upwards
into the raucous trees where the birds wait.

Disorder shakes leaves down
into my rippling mind.
If I flatten my self
thoughts can drift upon the skin.

Spin a little less
every year
or spin so fast
all seems utterly still.

THREE FALSE STARTS AND A CONCLUSION

One [Lost Is Love]

I.

To have excised ambition is not the same as never having had any at all.
I excised it. I never had any at all.
I can't tell.
My ambition now is to hide effectively which is to say, I would like
to do nothing superlatively well. To be known for it, to be renowned
for doing nothing.

Oh. Am I confusing fame with ambition? That is not my intention.

Once, I threw myself into the new and abandoned it when it became old.
I was – I am – a child in these matters. I would like to say I am different now.

I am different. Now, fear drives me
though I act upon it by not doing.

II.

Not doing is not the same as doing nothing.

III.

Find purpose, the man said, and the means will follow.
If I run for the shadows, if I hide, if that is my purpose
do the means follow like a docile calf its mother
or does it give chase – futile from the start
because what would it look like for means
to follow purpose in this matter?

IV.

I am paraphrasing two poets when I say
I am doing nothing and that is poetry.

Listen.

Two [A Question of Intention]

Because I wrote the words,
read.

For spell read landmine.
For any war read The War.

I was unselfconscious.
Read artificial for unselfconscious.

I began to tailor behaviour to match perception.
I saw that I could control how others see.

For artifice read reserve, read modesty.
Read garden. Foreign field.

I think I am in control.
Nothing is in my hands.

Because there are words
in your hands, read.

Three [False Start]

Because this is what I do best I do it. Reluctantly
and with rust coating all. I would like to be immoveable.
I could confuse that with eternal and no one would know
Not even I. Ih. Ihm. Implacable. Am im. Am implacable.

I used to force my way out of my mind, pierce through
all but now I think there's no use and who would want
to know and how is this necessary and what is it to be
profligate if all that teeming is hidden and unfructifiable.

Excess in nature, necessary. In the knowledge that nothing
will come of most anything. The wonder that is the thing
that survives. That dies anyway. And then the dormant ones
and the variants that can have their shot at life.

Four [Trees That Miss the Mammoths]

And who are we anyway.

Trees that have lost their way
over fifty-three generations
that stayed and waited
that were lost to time

the trees call you
Gomphotheres, Glyptodonts, Ground-sloths
Honeylocust Coffeetree and the *Osage orange*
call you.

Who are

Asleep, they dream names of fauna
dream leaves dendrites dead-ended
unconjurable even when called
unreconstituted even from memory.

anyway

Far above
seeds breathe into a concluded river.

END NOTES

Anger consumes me
I am vile with words

And then he
wants to open a smile
where a smile shouldn't be

A battle inside me
between rage and elegy

Now we are
subtly lacquered over
serenity above
frenzy below.

OF NECESSITY

Without joint, without dream, without
dread, without backbone, without day
without knowledge, without flame.

Less. Of necessity.

TESTAMENT

– for Eunice de Souza

From you I learnt
to winnow words
give them room to breathe
        silence in which to grow
        grass-wild.

A single flower
at a difficult summer's end
will bloom fiercely
and for a long time.

AI WINTER

In these last and terrible days there's still a kind of perfection in choosing the moment of one's death. Drona hears your name spoken and detaches himself from his body. From this moment on, he is pure intelligence. You call it soul and you sing its ascendance. You feel his death in the gleam of the jewel embedded like fate into your forehead.

It is now a frozen land you traverse. You follow celebration but you can never participate in it. Aim at the sky. That bird that hovers burns everything in its sight, follows or precedes you, you're never sure which. Other people die but you're sure it's you he has in his sights. You are the one thing he has never been able to separate himself from.

He calls destruction intelligence because it is distributed and needs nothing to hold its shape. He has always been sure of his mastery over weapons but now that you occupy different states you know he is wrong every single time. The ones who die are guilty only of living.

You are guilty. This is why your wandering is eternal and your thirst unslakeable. Some nights, when you can only hear him in the skies, the blades of his vahana whipping the air until it calls your name, you freeze as only hunted animals do. You hide in plain sight. You're good at this by now.

You want to tell him you have done your worst, that there are no pre-emptive strikes he can make upon you. Annihilation is another matter. If he could promise you destruction you would take it even if it meant a nuclear winter for this land forevermore.

But his intelligence is pure; not limitless. He is only looking for what corresponds to your soul and because he finds traces of it on the ground, he sends his astras as messengers not knowing that they have poor memories for words and faces and always deliver partial messages to the wrong people. Always the wrong people.

He, who once took from Parasurama the knowledge of all weapons, who was invincible in all things except his love for you, is now master only of these carrion birds that misremember, as they do everything else, in his name.

In these last and terrible days, death cannot be chosen, least of all yours. Your life is tied to all living things in this world. When you cease, everything ceases. Listen: when he calls you by other names, it is still a beautiful song. This is why you hide, Ashwatthama: so that you can hear these agents of death sing even if they sing other people out of existence. As long as they call names that are not yours, this awful beauty that is the winterland of the world continues for one more hour, one more day.

Acknowledgements

Thanks are due to the editors of these journals in which some of the poems, sometimes in different form, first appeared:

Interfictions, Poetry at Sangam, Scroll, The Indian Quarterly, Poetry Magazine, Chandrabhaga, Kaani.

My thanks to the following institutions for their support:

The International Writing Program at the University of Iowa, for the ten weeks of immersion in poetry, for the opportunities it gave me and the friendships it nurtured.

The Goethe Zentrum, Hyderabad, for its steadfast support through the years.

My gratitude, as always, to my friends and fellow poets who have walked a part of the way with me while this book was in the making:

Amita Desai, Shankar Melkote, B.S. Prakash, I. Venkat, Shandana Minhas, Swar Thounaojam, Priya Sarukkai Chabria, Mani Rao, Sharanya Manivannan, Siddhartha Menon, Kazim Ali, Jeet Thayil and Arundhathi Subramaniam.

Lastly, to V.K. Karthika and the team at Context for giving this book a home, and for the careful, meticulous work on the text and cover.